232

Merry Christm[...]

Love,
The HB1 Y[..] [...]

shine!

Library of Congress Cataloging-in-Publication Data
Dalton, Elaine S. (Elaine Schwartz), 1946– author.
  Shine! / Elaine S. Dalton.
    pages cm
  Summary: Elaine S. Dalton, the president of the Young Women organization of The Church of Jesus Christ of Latter-day Saints, shares her advice and counsel to the young women of the Church.
  Includes bibliographical references.
  ISBN 978-1-60907-224-7 (hardbound: alk. paper)
  1. Conduct of life. 2. Christian life—Mormon authors. 3. The Church of Jesus Christ of Latter-day Saints—Doctrines. 4. Young Women (The Church of Jesus Christ of Latter-day Saints) I. Title.
  BJ1589.D355 2012
  248.8'33—dc23   2012027569

Printed in the United States
Publishers Printing, Salt Lake City, Utah

10   9   8   7   6   5   4   3   2   1

shine!

ELAINE S. DALTON

DESERET
BOOK

SALT LAKE CITY, UTAH

To my mother, Emma Schwartz

*"Arise and shine forth,
that thy light may be a
standard for the nations."*

—Doctrine and Covenants 115:5

*T*his book has been in my heart for a long time. I suppose it all began in my childhood, when I would skip home from church with a tune in my mind that I just could not contain. I would sing it as I skipped along the sidewalk, and I loved each word:

> Jesus wants me for a sunbeam,
> To shine for him each day,
> In ev'ry way try to please him,
> At home, at school, at play.

Sometimes as I skipped home from church I wore a large gold star on my forehead. My teacher had put it there because I had behaved so well in her class. I loved my gold star. It seemed to make me feel even more committed to be a good girl and to be a sunbeam. I wanted to *shine* as brightly as the sun for Him because, even as a child, I loved the Savior.

Everywhere I go, it seems that I see young women *whose eyes shine with the light of the Spirit.* These young women know that they are daughters of our Heavenly Father. They are standing as witnesses and working to develop Christlike attributes. They are virtuous and pure, and they have the companionship of the Holy Ghost. Their inner goodness radiates in their eyes and in their faces. *They shine!* They are lights shining brightly in the world. And yet, they don't even realize that others notice.

You may not think anyone cares, but your Father in Heaven does. And I do! So this book is for you—*the young women who shine.* It is for my daughter, my daughters-in-law, my granddaughters, and young women everywhere who love the Savior and are striving to be like Him. It is for all young women who want to feel His love. I hope that as you read these pages, you will understand who you are and recognize your divine potential and destiny. You are elect. Your life matters and your choices matter and you matter!

As you *shine* with the light of the Savior and reflect His light to others, they will feel the warmth of His Spirit and His love. The more you do this, the brighter you'll *shine!*

$\mathcal{M}$y grandfather used to recite a poem to me when I was about your age. He said:

> You don't have to tell how you live each day;
> You don't have to tell if you work or play;
> A tried and true barometer stands in its place—
> You don't have to tell, it will show in your face. . . .
> If you live close to God and His infinite grace—
> You won't have to tell, it will show in your face.

I have never forgotten that simple poem, and I have always tried to live in such a way that light would show in my face. I can see that you are doing that also. The light in your countenance comes because you have made and kept covenants with our Heavenly Father and His Son, Jesus Christ, and you have made choices that qualify you to have the companionship of the Holy Ghost.

*P*resident Gordon B. Hinckley has said of you, "You are . . . the finest [and strongest] generation of young people ever in the history of this Church" (*Teachings of Gordon B. Hinckley* [1997], 714). I believe you have been prepared and reserved to be on the earth at this time when the challenges and opportunities are the greatest. I believe that the Lord is counting on you to be a leader for righteousness and to stand as a witness "at all times and in all things, and in all places" (Mosiah 18:9). Indeed, it can be said of you that you are the "bright shining hope" of the future (Gordon B. Hinckley, "Standing Strong and Immovable," *Worldwide Leadership Training Meeting*, Jan. 10, 2004, 20).

The Lord has blessed me with a very clear understanding of who you are and why you are here on the earth at this time. The Lord loves you, and I know you love Him. It shows in your countenance, in your modesty, in your desire to choose the right, and in your commitment to remain virtuous and pure.

I believe that you are included in those spoken of by the Apostle Peter when he said, "Ye are a chosen generation, a royal priesthood, an holy nation, a peculiar people; that ye should shew forth the praises of him who hath called you out of darkness into his marvellous light" (1 Peter 2:9).

That light is the Savior's light. It is the light of the restored gospel of Jesus Christ. By the way you live the gospel, you reflect His light. Your example will have a powerful effect for good on the earth. "Arise and shine forth, that thy light may be a standard for the nations" (Doctrine and Covenants 115:5) is a call to each of you. It is a call to move to higher ground. It is a call to leadership—to lead out in decency, purity, modesty, and holiness. It is a call to share this light with others.

It is time to "arise and shine forth."

When my daughter, Emi, was a little girl getting ready to go to church, I would comb her hair and put her pretty dress on her. Then she would say, "Let's put on our shiny." I had a jar of cosmetic cream that was clear and really did produce a shine. We would put it on her cheeks and on her lips, and then she would smile and say, "Let's go now, Mom."

What Emi didn't realize was that she already had her "shiny" on. Her face glowed because she was righteous and pure and because she had the Spirit with her—and it showed.

I wish every young woman would know that her beauty does not lie in makeup or hip clothing or the latest styles in hair or jewelry. *It lies in her righteousness.* Young women who are righteous and who have paid the price to be guided by the Holy Ghost and have Him for their constant companion can have a *powerful impact* in the world. You will be leaders of other young women who will see your "shiny" and want to be like you.

*Y*ou are young women of *great faith.* You brought your faith with you when you came to the earth. Alma teaches us that in the premortal realms you exhibited "exceeding faith and good works" (Alma 13:3). You fought with your faith and testimony to defend the plan that was presented by God. You knew the plan was good, and you knew that the Savior would do what He said He would do—because *you knew Him!* You stood with Him, and you were eager for your opportunity to come to earth. You knew what was going to be required of you. You knew it would be difficult, and yet you were confident not only that you could accomplish your divine mission but that you could make a difference. You are "choice spirits who were reserved to come forth in the fulness of times to take part in laying the foundations of the great latter-day work, including the building of the temples and the performance of ordinances therein" (Doctrine and Covenants 138:53–54).

And now you are here to do what you have been reserved and prepared to do.

President Thomas S. Monson has said of you:

*A*lthough there have always been challenges in the world, many of those which you face are unique to this time. But you are some of our Heavenly Father's *strongest* children, and He has saved you to come to the earth 'for such a time as this' (Esther 4:14). With His help, you will have the *courage* to face whatever comes. Though the world may at times appear dark, you have the *light* of the gospel, which will be as a *beacon* to guide your way" ("May You Have Courage," *Ensign*, May 2009, 127).

Can one righteous young woman change the world?

The answer is a resounding **"yes!"**

You have the Holy Ghost as your guide, and He "will show unto you all things . . . [you] should do" (2 Nephi 32:5). It is the daily, consistent things you do that will strengthen you to be a leader and an example—daily prayer, daily scripture study, daily obedience, daily service to others. As you do these things, you will grow closer to the Savior and become more and more like Him. As with Moses and Abinadi and other faithful leaders (see Exodus 34:30; Mosiah 13:5; Matthew 17:1-2), your face will glow with the fire of your faith.

"By small and simple things are great things brought to pass" (Alma 37:6).

I am amazed at the way little things, done daily and consistently, really do add up! You can make a difference in your own happiness, in your home, and with your friends. You are leaders.

I think it is time to sparkle.

My definition of *sparkle* is an inward understanding that shows on the outside. Here's what I mean:

S   Smile and remember that you are a daughter of God

P   Pray every day

A   Attitude—be positive, look for the good

R   Read in the Book of Mormon five minutes each day

K   Keep the commandments

L   Live the standards with exactness

E   Example—be an example of the believers

Sparkle! Let your light shine so that others will want to follow your example.

Our granddaughter, Ella, understood this principle of "sparkle" at an early age. She wrote the following poem when she was just seven years old:

Sparkle!

Once my younger sister and I bought some sparkle spray
at the beauty store. We loved putting it on all over our bodies,
especially our cheeks and foreheads.
People probably noticed that it was just artificial.

If you are wearing sparkle spray, people can still tell
that it's just artificial.

What is on the outside doesn't matter
as much as what is on the inside—
your personality,
your kind heart,
your mind.

A big house doesn't matter.
Fancy clothes aren't all that important either.

Sparkles are beautiful, especially sparkles that are inside.
If you are good, you will sparkle.
People who help are sparkly.
You can see it in their eyes.

You see that someone sparkles by how they act.
Sparkles come out by helping.
They come out of your heart.
Your eyes will shine.
Your words will be kind.
Your hands will help.
Your mind will tell you what is right and
Your heart will help you act on it.
Your feet will carry you to the right place.

So, come on! Just sparkle!

Ella and Louisa

A few days after Ella was baptized, she let out a loud scream in her bathroom. Her mother ran to see what had happened. There stood Ella in front of the mirror in tears.

Her mother said, "What is the matter?"

Ella replied tearfully, *"I have lost my sparkle!"*

Her mother asked her if she had done anything since she was baptized that would cause her to lose her sparkle.

She bowed her head and said, "Well, I have been mean to my little sister Louisa."

So Ella repented. She went to Louisa and said she was sorry, and then she noticed that her sparkle had returned. Even little Ella knew that the gift of the Holy Ghost changes your appearance.

I have seen "sparkle" in the countenances of young women around the world. The faces of the young women in West Africa shine with the *radiant light* of the Holy Ghost. They live the standards in the *For the Strength of Youth* pamphlet, they are guided by the Spirit, and they are preparing to be leaders. They love the Lord and are grateful for His light in their lives. Some of these young women walked three hours to share their testimonies with me. Because of them, I will never be the same.

When I was in South America, the young women and their leaders sang, "I'm Trying to Be like Jesus." They didn't just sing the words; they meant what they sang. In Asia and India, young women are *examples* of faith, modest dress, and purity. Their eyes shine, and they are happy. The young women in England, Ireland, and Wales are standing for truth and righteousness in their schools. In an ever-darkening world, they are making a difference.

Some of you are the only members of the Church in your family or your school. You are making a difference. You are leading in righteous ways.

This is a magnificent time to be on the earth and to be a young woman. Our vision remains the same as it has always been: It is to be worthy to make and keep sacred covenants and receive the ordinances of the temple. This is our superlative goal! And so we will continue to do all we can to help each other *"stand in holy places"* (Doctrine and Covenants 45:32) and receive, recognize, and rely on the Holy Ghost.

We will continue to talk of Christ, to rejoice in Christ, that each of us will know to what source we may look for a remission of our sins (see 2 Nephi 25:26). And yes, we will continue to *stand firm* no matter what storms may rage around us because we know and testify that "it is upon the rock of our Redeemer, who is Christ, the Son of God, that [we] must build [our] foundation . . . , a foundation whereon if [we] build [we] cannot fall" (Helaman 5:12).

The Lord's counsel to Joshua is His counsel to you today:

"Be strong and of a good courage; be not afraid, neither be thou dismayed: for the Lord thy God is with thee whithersoever thou goest" (Joshua 1:9).

You are not alone!

Though you may be the only Latter-day Saint in your school or your group of friends or even your family, you are not alone. You can rely on the strength of the Lord. As Joshua said to the Israelites, "Sanctify yourselves: for to morrow the Lord will do wonders among you" (Joshua 3:5). This was Joshua's call for a return to virtue, and it is the same call to us today. We simply cannot do the work we have been reserved and prepared to do unless we can access the strength and confidence that comes by living a virtuous life.

*Y*oung women of The Church of Jesus Christ of Latter-day Saints, *remember who you are!* You are elect. You are daughters of God. You cannot be a generation of young women who are content to fit in. You must have the courage to *stand out.* The world would have you believe that you are not significant—that you are out of fashion and out of touch. The world calls to you with unrelenting, noisy voices to "live it up," "try everything," "experiment and be happy." Conversely, the Holy Ghost whispers and the Lord invites you to "walk in the paths of virtue," "lay aside the things of this world," "and cleave unto [your] covenants" (Doctrine and Covenants 25:2, 10, 13).

The world will tell you that you are not acceptable, that you are lacking. It will tell you that you are not enough—rich enough, pretty enough, skinny enough, or cool enough.

But the Lord will tell you that you are acceptable, that, because of His Son's Atonement, you are enough. He wants you to be happy and growing and becoming all that He intended you to become. Right now you are *becoming*—it is a time of growth and discovery and learning. It is the time for you to prepare for your future roles as wives, mothers, and homemakers. You have all that you need to fulfill your divine destiny because you have the companionship of the Holy Ghost. You have the scriptures; you know how to pray. You have parents and leaders who love you and will help you. You know who you are—daughters of God. You know where you are going. *You can do it.*

I have always loved the story of the son of King Louis XVI of France because he had an unshakable knowledge of his identity. As a young man, he was kidnapped by evil men who had dethroned his father, the king. These men knew that if they could destroy him morally, he could not be heir to the throne. For six months they subjected him to every vile thing life had to offer, and yet he never yielded under pressure. This puzzled his captors. After doing everything they could think of, they asked him why he had such great moral strength. His reply was simple. He said, "I cannot do what you ask, for I was born to be a king" (see Vaughn Featherstone, "The King's Son," *New Era*, November 1975, 35).

Like the king's son, each of you has inherited a royal birthright. Each of you has a *divine heritage.* As President Ezra Taft Benson said, "You are literally the royal daughters of our Father in Heaven" ("To the Young Women of the Church," *Ensign*, November 1986, 85). Each of you was *born to be a queen.*

When I was attending Brigham Young University, I learned what it truly means to be a queen. I was given an unusual opportunity, along with a small group of other students, to meet the prophet, President David O. McKay. I was told to wear my best dress and to be ready to travel early the next morning to Huntsville, Utah, to the home of the prophet. I will never forget the experience I had. As soon as we entered, I felt the spirit that filled that home. We were seated in the prophet's living room, surrounding him. President McKay had on a white suit, and seated next to him was his wife. He asked for each of us to come forward and tell him about ourselves. As I went forward, he held out his hand and held mine, and as I told him about my life and my family, he looked deeply into my eyes.

After we had finished, he leaned back in his chair and reached for his wife's hand and said, "Now, young women, I would like you to meet *my queen.*"

There seated next to him was his wife, Emma Ray McKay. Although she did not wear a crown of sparkling diamonds, nor was she seated on a throne, I *knew* she was a true queen. Her white hair was her crown, and her pure eyes sparkled like jewels. As President and Sister McKay spoke of their family and their life together, their intertwined hands spoke volumes about their love. Joy radiated from their faces. Hers was a beauty that cannot be purchased. It came from years of seeking the best gifts, becoming well educated, seeking knowledge by study and also by faith. It came from years of working hard, of faithfully enduring trials with optimism, trust, strength, and courage. It came from her unwavering devotion and fidelity to her husband, her family, and the Lord.

On that fall day in Huntsville, Utah, I was reminded of my divine identity, and I learned about what I now call "deep beauty"—the kind of beauty

that shines from the inside out. It is the kind of beauty that cannot be painted on, surgically created, or purchased. It is the kind of beauty that doesn't wash off. It is *spiritual* attractiveness.

Deep beauty springs from virtue. It is the beauty of being chaste and morally clean. It is the kind of beauty that you see in the eyes of virtuous women like your mother and grandmother. It is a beauty that is earned through faith, repentance, and honoring covenants.

*T*he world places its emphasis on physical attractiveness. It would have you believe that you are to look like the illusive model on the cover of a magazine. The Lord would tell you that you are each *uniquely beautiful.* When you are virtuous, chaste, and morally clean, your inner beauty glows in your eyes and in your face. When you are worthy of the companionship of the Holy Ghost, you are confident and your *inner beauty shines* brightly. And so "let virtue garnish thy thoughts unceasingly; then shall thy confidence wax strong in the presence of God; and . . . the Holy Ghost shall be thy constant companion" (Doctrine and Covenants 121:45–46).

Recently, a group of young women visited my office. At the end of the visit, one young woman confided with tears in her eyes, "I have never thought of myself as beautiful. I have always felt very ordinary. But today, as I walked past the mirror in your office and glanced into it, I was beautiful!" She *was* beautiful because her face shone with the Spirit. She saw herself as our Heavenly Father sees her. She had received His image in her countenance. That is deep beauty.

Young women, look into the mirror of eternity. *Remember who you are!* See yourself as our Heavenly Father sees you. You are elect. You are of noble birth. Don't compromise your divine inheritance. You were born to be a queen.

Live so you are worthy to enter the temple and there receive "all that [the] Father hath" (Doctrine and Covenants 84:38). Develop deep beauty. There is no more beautiful sight than a young woman who glows with the light of the Spirit, who is confident and courageous because she is virtuous.

Remember, you are daughters of our Heavenly Father. He loves you so much that He sent His Son to show you the way to live, so that you could return to Him someday. I testify that as you draw close to the Savior, His infinite Atonement makes it possible for you to repent, to change, to be pure, and to receive *His image in your countenance.*

*N*ot so long ago, I hiked with a group of youth to the top of Ensign Peak. There we looked out at the city of Salt Lake and the temple and talked of the sacrifice so many had made for the gospel. Then each of the youth unfurled a banner. On their banners they had drawn symbols of their message to the world—what they wanted to stand for in these latter days. It was thrilling to hear the commitment and testimony of each one. Then we sang "High on the Mountain Top" and the youth cheered together, "Hurrah for Israel!" (see Orson F. Whitney, *Life of Heber C. Kimball* [1945], 266). I echo those words here. *Hurrah for you!*

I hope you will never hesitate to "let your light so shine . . . that [others will] see your good works, and glorify your Father which is in heaven" (Matthew 5:16). I hope you too will raise your banners high. I know that as you lead in righteousness, this scripture in Isaiah will be fulfilled: "For, behold, . . . the Lord shall arise upon thee, and his glory shall be seen upon thee" (Isaiah 60:2). It will be discernible, and "the Gentiles shall come to thy light, and kings to the brightness of thy rising" (Isaiah 60:3).

I can see a day when the world will look to you and say: "Who are you? Who are these young women who radiate this light? Why are you so happy? How do you know your direction in such a confusing world?" And you will arise and stand on your feet and say with conviction:

"We are daughters of our Heavenly Father, who loves us, and we love Him."

—Young Women Theme

Sometimes it may seem almost impossible to keep shining. You encounter so many challenges that may obscure the source of all light, which is the Savior. Sometimes the way is difficult, and it may even seem at times that a thick fog obscures the light.

Such was the case with a young woman named Florence Chadwick. From the age of 10, Florence discovered that she was a talented swimmer. She swam the English Channel in a record time of 13 hours and 20 minutes. Florence loved a challenge, and she later attempted to swim between the coastline of California and Catalina Island—some 21 miles (34 km). On this swim she grew weary after swimming 15 hours. A thick fog set in that obscured the view of the coastline. Her mother was riding alongside her in a boat, and Florence told her mother that she didn't think she could finish. Her mother and her trainer encouraged her to continue, but all she could see was the fog. She abandoned her swim, but once inside the boat, she discovered she had quit within one mile (1.6 km) of the coastline. Later, when she was interviewed and asked why she had abandoned her swim, she confessed that it wasn't the cold water and it wasn't the distance. She said, "I was licked by the fog" (see Sterling W. Sill, in Conference Report, April 1955, 117).

Later she attempted the swim again, and once more, a thick fog set in. But this time, she kept going until she successfully reached the coastline. This time when she was asked what made the difference, she said that she kept a mental image of the coastline in her mind through the thick fog and throughout the duration of her swim (see Randy Alcom, "Florence Chadwick and the Fog," epm.org/resources/2010/Jan/21/florence-chadwick-and-fog).

For Florence Chadwick, the coastline was her goal. For each of us, the temple is our goal. Young women, stay focused. Don't lose sight of your goals. Don't let the thick fog of moral pollution and the detracting voices of the world keep you from reaching your goals, living the standards, enjoying the companionship of the Holy Ghost, and being worthy to enter holy temples.

Retain the vision of the temple—the Savior's holy house—ever in your hearts and minds.

From my window in the Young Women office, I have a spectacular view of the Salt Lake Temple. Every day I see the angel Moroni standing atop the temple as a shining symbol of not only his faith but ours. I love Moroni because, in a very degenerate society, he remained pure and true. He is my hero. He stood alone. I feel somehow he stands atop the temple today, beckoning us to have courage, to remember who we are, and to be worthy to enter the holy temple—to "arise and shine forth" (Doctrine and Covenants 115:5), to stand above the worldly clamor, and to, as Isaiah prophesied, "Come... to the mountain of the Lord" (Isaiah 2:3)—the holy temple.

*M*y call to you is the same as Moroni's call: "Awake, and arise . . . , O daughter[s] of Zion" (Moroni 10:31). He saw you. He saw this day. These are your days! I believe that as you awake and arise, your light will be a standard to the nations, but I also believe your standards will be a light to the nations.

The call to "arise and shine forth" is a call to each of you to *lead the world* in a mighty cause—to raise the standard—and lead this generation in virtue, purity, and temple worthiness. If you desire to make a difference in the world, *you must be different from the world.* I echo the words of President Joseph F. Smith, who said to the women of his day: "It is not for you to be led by the [young] women of the world; it is for you to lead . . . the [young] women of the world, in everything that is . . . purifying to the children of men" (*Teachings of Presidents of the Church: Joseph F. Smith* [1998], 184). These words ring true today.

*A*s daughters of God, you were born to lead.

You are set apart. You distinguished yourselves in the premortal existence. Your lineage carries with it covenants and promises. You have inherited the spiritual attributes of the faithful—even Abraham, Isaac, and Jacob.

Your very nature reflects your *divine heritage* and destiny. The fact that you were born a girl is not by chance. Your divine characteristics will be magnified as you lead others and live up to your divine potential.

*A*nd so I conclude with the Lord's words to each of us, His precious daughters: "Behold, . . . thou art an elect lady, whom I have called" (Doctrine and Covenants 25:3). "Keep my commandments continually, and a *crown of righteousness* thou shalt receive" (Doctrine and Covenants 25:15).

Draw close to the Savior. He lives! He is the light, life, and hope of the world. He will lead you and give you courage to share your light. What my grandfather taught me was true: "When you live close to God and His infinite grace, you won't have to tell, it will show in your face." My prayer is that you will always remember to *shine!*

Photo Credits